Getting Your Voice to Shake:

A Practical Guide to Intercultural Communication

Kelly Nix

Getting Your Voice to Shake: A Practical Guide to Intercultural Communication

By Kelly Nix

©2016 Kelly Nix
   San Antonio, Texas 78250

ISBN-13: 978-1541002661
ISBN-10: 1541002660

Contents

Preface... 7

Chapter 1: Learning to Fit In.................................... 9

Chapter 3: Sticking Together 29

Chapter 4: I Know What You Said...But What Did You Mean?.. 37

Chapter 5: Time Travel 49

Chapter 6: That's the Only Face You Have – Don't Lose It!... 63

Chapter 7: Keep Your Distance!............................ 73

Chapter 8: Signing Off.. 87

Bibliography.. 91

Dedication

To my wife, Valerie. Thanks for 25 wonderful years. May the next 50 or so be just as good!

Preface

Words are powerful. To borrow a quote from Scripture, "death and life are in the power of the tongue." And as someone who was raised between two cultures and who enjoys two distinct national identities, I've seen a lot of conflict as different cultures clash. My firm belief is that we must do a better job of talking to each other.

Unraveling the mysteries of communicating effectively across cultural lines is key in today's world of global business and travel. I hope this book will serve as an important first step developing awareness of the very real differences in how people from different cultures perceive the same realities, and that it will help all of my readers take a big step up the ladder toward becoming expert intercultural communicators. In so doing, they will develop valuable skills that will no doubt be invaluable to their careers – and in the process, they just might gain a whole lot of new friends!

Kelly Nix
San Antonio, Texas
December 7, 2016

Chapter 1: Learning to Fit In

"Breaker-one-nine...you got your ears on?"

Back in the 1970s and 1980s, when I was a kid, the CB radio craze was alive and well in America.

Then, as now, professional truck drivers used CBs as a necessary tool for sharing information as they crisscrossed the country. But CB use wasn't limited to commercial drivers. Oh, no... "four-wheelers" (to the uninitiated, cars) had them too. And what was a practical tool for the truckers was a source of fascination and fun for the rest of us – and did we ever love to use it!

There were people who got on the CB and tried to talk in ordinary language...a cardinal sin that no doubt set eyes rolling in vehicles for miles around. What were they thinking?? You couldn't just speak plain English on a CB radio...you had to know the "lingo!"

There was a code for everything. In fact, I remember laboring to memorize a CB code sheet with dozens of numbers. Who wanted to ask "What time is it?" when you could go on the air and request a 10-36? Or ask "Where are you?" when instead you could say, "What's your 20?"

After awhile, though, if you learned the code, the conversations on the radio started to make sense. But to someone who was listening without the benefit of a code sheet, it was pure nonsense. They might well know all the words because they spoke English – but in the particular *context* in which those words were used, they would make no sense whatsoever.

For example, you might have known what "local" and "yokel" meant; but how were you to know that, on the CB, those two words together referred to a city police officer? Or that a "County Mountie" was a sheriff...or that Smokey Bear was not a bear at all, but a highway patrolman waiting to invite you over to the shoulder for a chat about the laws of physics and the speed at which your vehicle was progressing?

Just a few minutes of listening to the on-air chatter would be enough to prove a very important point: it takes more than knowing the vocabulary of a language to actually communicate. Language skills are important to us understanding each other, but so is the context that gives meaning to the words we use. In the world of communication (particularly when it involves people from significantly different backgrounds), the framework that gives us context and other relevant factors is our culture.

People who have a shared culture – the "in-group" – tend to exchange messages with each other that go beyond the mere words they speak. Along with their speech they use important non-verbal cues such as body language to convey meaning. Getting into people's in-group can be difficult – or, in some cases, impossible; but the more access you are able to gain to their group, the better your chances will be of successfully communicating with them.

Case in point: I was born into a missionary family. My parents and two of my brothers were born in the United States; my other brother and I were born in Peru, where our family was stationed. Most of my childhood was spent overseas, though we would return to the States once every four years to spend a year or so traveling and promoting the work we were doing on the mission field.

Those years of traveling are fond memories for me. We were known as the "Nix Six," and we traveled all over the U.S. and Canada, often covering thousands of miles a week. During those trips we lived in a motorhome pulling a travel trailer – a vehicle nearly as long as the semi trucks with which we shared the road. And of course we had the inevitable CB radio.

Getting a CB was as easy as buying one and installing it. Getting professional drivers to converse with you, however, was a bit more challenging. Their "amateur detectors" worked amazingly well. One day, though, my older brother discovered the secret to "raising" truck drivers on the radio, and it worked almost invariably.

The principle behind this secret is powerful. In fact, you might even say that *it is the key to establishing communication with people outside our own "in-groups."*

My brother's revelation came from listening to truckers converse with each other. He noticed there was something telltale about truck drivers' voices that identified them as big rig drivers without them having to say so. What was the giveaway? Their voices shook when they talked!

It wasn't hard to figure out why. The suspension on semi trucks (especially back in the 70s!) is no doubt designed first for efficiency in hauling heavy loads, with the comfort of the drivers as a secondary consideration. Driving a truck, from the sound of it, must be a pretty bouncy job!

So my brother worked on getting his voice to shake. Not only did he imitate the vocabulary and speech *style* of the drivers, but he inserted shakiness in his voice as a non-verbal cue that would signal to drivers that he was one of them, doing what they did. And it worked! He didn't just know the right words – he actually sounded like he belonged. After figuring out this trick, he was able to hold many conversations with an audience that otherwise might not have accepted him.

What I just described is exactly the type of approach that can help you communicate effectively with people from other cultures. In the rest of this book I'll take information gleaned from respected experts in the field of intercultural communication and mix it with things I learned on my own by growing up transitioning among many cultures. I've also done some formal research on my own that backs up the opinions of the experts. In fact, if you want to read more about the technical side of things, check out my book *Intercultural Communication in Business*[1] – but I warn you...it's a research project, not a novel.

It's a given that cross-cultural communication requires sharing a common language, and I certainly encourage people to learn to speak more than one language.

I'm fluent in three, and if I can do it, I assure you that pretty much anyone can if they work at it. But just knowing the same set of words your audience knows and being able to string them together in grammatically correct sequences is not enough. Remember: *If you want to converse with truckers, you have to get your voice to shake.*

It's worth noting that the ability to communicate is something people have been studying for a long time. Way back in 1949, two researchers named Claude Shannon and Warren Weaver developed a model of communication that includes the following elements: an *information source* (the person sending the message), an *encoder* (the device or object that encodes the message into signals), a *channel* (to which the signals are adapted for transmission), a *decoder* (the device or object that converts the received signals into a message), and a *destination* (the recipient of the signal). Along the way, the signals passing through the channel may be subject to *noise*, which may lead to the received signal being different from what was sent.[2]

In the case of intercultural communication, we can apply the Shannon-Weaver Model as follows: an information source (you); an encoder (your mouth, your computer, etc.); a channel (a verbal conversation; a phone conversation; communication via text, email, chat, etc.); a decoder (the other person's ear, computer screen, etc.); and a destination (the person you are addressing). The specific type of "noise" or static we are going to address consists of cultural differences that can cause people to misunderstand each other.

If you are one of the many people who are finding today's world to be a lot smaller than it used to be and you wish you could break through the barriers that make it hard to communicate with people from other cultures, you're in luck. In the next few chapters I'll share a few simple but powerful secrets that can help take the mystery out of intercultural communication. Ready? Let's go!

Chapter 2: Stereotypes Are Bad...Aren't They?

There's no question that it's becoming increasingly difficult to make cultural generalizations. The face of America – and of our world – is rapidly changing in response to our relatively newfound ability to move around the globe with ease. Societies and cultures that used to know about each other primarily by reading books about faraway lands are now bumping into each other on the sidewalk on a regular basis.

My wife and I are great examples of the inadequacy of outdated cultural stereotypes. She is of Hispanic descent, but born and raised in the United States. I am of Anglo-American descent, but born in Peru and raised in various locations across South, Central and North America. Many people assume she is from Latin America and I am from the States – the exact opposite of the truth! So while our physical characteristics might push us into familiar boxes, our fit in those boxes might be uncomfortable.

Nevertheless, to assume there is no value in cultural generalizations would be a serious mistake. While there will always be individuals within cultures who do not fit the broader cultural mold, many ethnic, regional and national people groups *do* share a broad range of habits and characteristics, and recognizing these makes it much easier to learn how to communicate.

Not every American from the South says "y'all." In fact, I don't doubt that some of them are offended by such a grammatical atrocity. But despite my own South American origins, my family tree has deep roots in Arkansas, Texas and Tennessee...and to convince me that saying "y'all" is not a valid cultural generalization for *most* – though certainly not all – Southerners would be a hard task indeed. Besides, I kind of like saying it. Okay, y'all?

So while it is disingenuous and potentially harmful to try impose a cultural generalization or stereotype on every individual, generalizations can be very helpful when you are trying to understand a culture at large. And when you are learning to communicate effectively across cultures, generalizations can help you get that "shake in your voice" that will take you from merely adequate to exceptional and effective as an intercultural communicator.

If you study cultural anthropology and how it affects communication, names like Hall, Gudykunst, Trompenaars, Hampden-Turner, Hofstede, Morrison, Conaway and Storti are probably very familiar to you. Each of these authors (and many others) have made valuable contributions to the field of intercultural communication. In my doctoral studies, I performed independent research to verify whether their conclusions were reliable – and they were. So rather than reinvent the wheel, I'm going to draw on their research to help you understand what I believe are the most critical elements of successfully communicating with people from other cultures.

Before I do that, though, I do want to stress one very important thing. All technical and anthropological issues aside, *respect for other people's culture* is, in my opinion, the cornerstone of good communication. By no means do you have to agree with every aspect of someone's culture, but it is essential that you recognize that your culture and theirs are equally valuable. Avoiding the trap of *ethnocentricity* (the belief that one's own culture is superior to others) will help you immensely in your efforts to bridge the culture gap.

For example, suggesting to someone from China or from Israel that they read "backward" because they read from right-to-left instead of left-to-right will likely be amusing to them (if they have a good sense of humor) or offensive to them (if they don't). To them, *you* are the one who reads backward. Who is right?

When it comes to culture, "different" is not necessarily wrong – it's just different. Don't waste your time trying to turn someone from another culture into an

American (or Canadian, or Australian, or Chinese, or Brazilian, or Angolan, or Russian, or Sri Lankan, or whatever your own culture of origin may be). That expresses to them that you feel their culture is somehow less desirable than yours. It's also an exercise in futility – most people I've encountered are not really interested in trading their birth culture for another.

Instead, seek to learn how to communicate with them *within* their culture as someone who is equal but different. When it comes to cultures, different can be awesome!

Chapter 3: Sticking Together

"All for one and one for all" brings to mind Alexandre Dumas' *The Three Musketeers*. And while the phrase is iconic in literature, sadly the concept is a bit quaint in light of modern American culture.

"Every man for himself" is probably a bit closer to the way American culture works. I know, I know – you're probably thinking of several people you know who are not like that at all. Remember, though, that we are using generalizations, and not every individual will fit. Despite the exceptions, the generalization is fairly accurate.

In America (and no doubt much of the Western world), it's not unusual to not even know your next door neighbor's name. This is less true in rural settings, but very common in urban areas.

The culture of the United States – and of many other North American and Western European nations – is classified by cultural anthropologists as "individualistic." That means people's identity is derived primarily from the individual and secondarily from larger societal groups. This does not mean Americans do not care about anyone but themselves – quite the contrary. Many Americans are loving, caring and generous people. But they tend to see themselves *first* as individuals, and the prevailing philosophy is that individual success will ultimately equal national success.

In individualistic cultures, then, there is pressure – not surprisingly – for people to succeed as individuals. Having worked for many years in corporate America, I can attest that the "dog-eat-dog" workplace is not a myth, and that there is indeed a drive to climb the corporate ladder toward individual success, regardless of whose fingers might be stepped on along the way. Again, certainly not everyone in the American workplace fits this generalization, but many people do.

Please bear in mind that I am not judging cultures in this book. My purpose is not to extol or condemn. I am a proud American *and* a proud citizen of Peru – two very different cultures. What I *am* trying to do is point out proven cultural characteristics that explain why we behave as we do.

Rugged individualism has much to do with North America's rise to global prominence. The entrepreneurial spirit and the dogged belief that any man or woman can succeed in America if they try hard enough have together created countless cases of rags to riches. But the same attributes that have created the American success story can also become major obstacles to intercultural communication if we fail to understand that some cultures view identity and the individual's connection to society very differently.

Throughout Latin America and parts of Africa, Europe and Asia, one prevailing cultural factor is known as *collectivism*. This has nothing to do with politics or communism; what it refers to is the fact that people there tend to identify first as part of a group, and only secondarily as individuals.

To illustrate how this might affect behavior, allow me to share an anecdote. At one point in my career I oversaw a team of professionals scattered around the world. Most of their countries were culturally collectivist. Our U.S.-based teams decided to promote one of these individuals to a supervisory position.

My experience in corporate America taught me that such promotions were generally met with elation by the lucky employees, who were thrilled at the forward step in their careers. But this particular employee reacted in a way that would be incomprehensible in an individualistic culture. He contacted me and expressed his gratitude for the opportunity, but he also voiced a concern. "How do you think the other team members will feel about this?"

The employee did ultimately accept the position, but his self-deprecating behavior and constant regard for the others on the team made him not just a supervisor, but a beloved friend, mentor and confidant.

One very important thing to remember is that individualistic societies tend to put business before human relations, while collectivist societies value people first and business second. This affects many aspects of behavior and communication, and we'll discuss these further in upcoming chapters. It can also cause deep frustrations if people from one culture fail to understand the cultural values of others.

Chapter 4: I Know What You Said...But What Did You Mean?

You're a nut!

Depending on the situation, you might be very angry with me over that assessment – particularly if I had a scowl on my face and was shaking my head and rolling my eyes in disgust when I said it. But if I was laughing hysterically at a humorous observation you had just made, you might consider it a high compliment to your comedic talents.

So *what* we say is important, but *how* we say it is equally important. The situation and the setting provide non-verbal information that can completely alter the way we understand spoken or written communication. We call this *context*, and it's one of the most important things you will need to understand if you want your voice to shake.

There are some cultures that rely heavily on context to convey the full meaning of what is said or written. We call these cultures *high-context*. Other cultures have very little reliance on context, preferring instead to be very detailed and explicit in what is stated. Unsurprisingly, these cultures are called *low-context*.

As a rule of thumb, collectivist cultures tend to be high-context, and individualistic cultures are more low-context. This has everything to do with how intercultural communication works!

North Americans are generally very direct. They say exactly what they mean, and they mean what they say. This is not considered rude in American society. Work-related emails are often very detailed, spelling out exactly what the writer hopes to communicate, with little effort wasted on niceties. But to a high-context reader, this could be a bit shocking.

For example, an email in the United States might read, "Hi Bob, How are things coming with the Acme deal?" In Latin America, though, the same email would likely start off something like this: "My most esteemed friend Bob, I hope this message finds you and your beautiful family well and enjoying good health. Forgive me for imposing on your very busy schedule, but when it is convenient would you kindly share with me the status of the valuable deal you are working on with Acme Corporation?"

Where directness and conciseness are valued in low-context cultures (remember: low-context cultures are generally individualistic, and individualistic cultures tend to value business over human relations), the opposite is true in high-context societies. It might be unthinkably rude to jump right to the point and get down to business without first thoroughly and elaborately expressing your appreciation for the person to whom you are writing. Americans often see this as nothing more than flowery speech – but it is an essential touch in a culture that values people over business. What better way to get off to a bad start than to let your reader know they really don't matter to you as a person?

It is also considered rude in many cases to make direct observations in a high-context situation. Rather than bluntly state something that might be embarrassing to either the hearer or the speaker, communicators may resort to vague and evasive language, with the expectation that the hearer will be culturally adept enough to figure out the true meaning.

High-context communicators often expect you to read between the lines, so they may use simple expressions that can be full of hidden meaning that you are supposed to be able to understand from what was said. For example, in some Latin American countries speakers will briefly stick out their tongue to indicate that what they just said was a joke.

Non-verbal communication is critical, and gestures play an important role in high-context communication. People from these cultures often use their hands as much as their mouths to express themselves. Other body language is important, too; for example, a backward nod in some Latin American countries can mean that the speaker is referring to something in the past, and, for Brazilians, a repeated snapping of the fingers can indicate that you are talking about something that happened a very long time ago.

Other gestures carry a lot of meaning as well. In many cultures it is offensive to call someone by waving back toward the speaker with the fingers pointed upward, as we do in America. Instead, the hand should be extended and the fingers pointed downward and then curled back toward the speaker. In some Middle Eastern cultures it is considered demeaning to point the bottom of your shoe toward someone, so you must exercise caution when crossing your legs. It is also offensive in many countries to shake hands or eat using your left hand, because that hand is used for personal hygiene.

People in high-context, collectivist cultures generally have great respect for hierarchy and authority, so the idea of telling someone "no" – particularly if that person is a superior – can be unthinkable. Instead, they might say that what is being asked would be "difficult." Or, they might wordlessly accept an assignment, believing that it must surely be obvious to the person making the request that it's not really feasible, but not wanting to embarrass them by pointing that out. When the assignment is not completed or the deadline met, the low-context requestor is often furious at having been let down, while the high-context person cannot comprehend the other person's anger at what should never truly have been expected to be accomplished in the first place.

If you are a low-context person assigning a task to someone from a high-context culture, you should be aware that anything other than an enthusiastic "Yes, that can be done" might be a signal intended to politely let you know you should not wait standing up, because it's probably not going to happen. If that's the case, you might tactfully request that the person give you some suggestions on what might be the best way to accomplish the task, or let you know whether it's really feasible at all.

Another example of a politely indirect refusal is Mexico's famous phrase, *primero*

Dios ("God first," or more generally, "God willing"). Because Mexico is a high-context, collectivist society that assigns a high value to people, an outright refusal would be very impolite – but you should understand that what "primero Dios" really means (generally speaking) is more like "ain't gonna happen." For some reason, every time I've been told "primero Dios," God apparently wasn't willing!

When my wife and I were learning Portuguese in Brazil, our language teacher told us that lunch engagements were only considered to be firm if they were reconfirmed after they were scheduled. If someone invited you to lunch but never called you to reaffirm the date, you had best not go unless you wanted to eat by yourself. To a foreigner, this would create an awkward situation – but a local would have known the engagement was off and would not have bothered to make the trip. That was clearly communicated...in a high-context way.

So, when you are communicating across cultural lines, pay close attention to what is said. But if you want to get that "shake in your voice" that makes you a truly great communicator, pay even closer attention to what *isn't* said.

Chapter 5: Time Travel

What time is it, anyway?

Wait – we're talking about intercultural communication. So before I ask you what time it is, perhaps I should first ask you what *kind* of time it is.

Are you surprised? Many people aren't aware there *is* more than one kind of time. And that's one of the primary sources of frustration when cultures encounter each other.

Let's introduce a couple of new words to our vocabulary. One is *monochronic*, and the other is *polychronic*. Before you think I'm really smart for coming up with such impressive terms, let me confess they're not mine at all – I borrowed them from the work of cultural anthropologist Edward Hall.[3]

In monochronic cultures, people tend to do things in a very linear fashion – one thing at a time. (Note: don't confuse *monochronic* with *monochromic*, which refers to something with only one color – you'd be amazed at how many of my students do!) The beginning of one task depends on the completion of the previous one, so people in monochronic cultures are very sensitive about punctuality.

You probably already figured this out, but the United States, Canada and parts of Western

Europe are monochronic societies. If you are going to be more than five minutes late for a social engagement in the U.S., you are expected to call the party you are meeting and let them know. And to be late for a business appointment is unthinkable.

When monochronic people feel their time has been disrespected, they often become irritated or even angry. This is because one schedule mishap can throw the remainder of their day off balance – and, after all, "time is money." At least, that's how we perceive it in North America.

Therefore, when a North American or Western European finds themselves in a polychronic society – or even dealing with polychronic people in their own society – the potential for conflict is abundant. Why, they fret, are people *persistently* late for appointments? Why does it seem they are not even aware of the clock?

It's not that they aren't aware; most likely, they are just as aware of the clock as you. It's just that they have a completely different perception of time than monochronic people. This different way of looking at time is what causes them to behave differently toward it.

The term *polychronic* refers to people who are not linear in their view of time. Where the monochronic individual does one thing at a time and is governed by a schedule, the polychronic person does many things at the same time, making it less important that any one of those things begin or end at a specific time. Polychronic people are mostly found in collectivist societies, and the view that people are more important than business is a strong factor in time perception; therefore, people come before schedules. In fact, Hall observes that "polychronic people...interact with several people at once and are continually involved with each other" and that "tight scheduling is therefore difficult, if not impossible."[4]

Hall uses the example of a monochronic customer with a polychronic hairdresser, and states that this will inevitably lead to problems because the monochronic customer will schedule appointments based on time constraints, while the polychronic hairdresser will always squeeze other VIP customers (such as friends and family) in. Why? You guessed it. People are more important than schedules. In fact, Hall writes that "the more important the customer or business that is disrupted, the more reassured the hairdresser's polychronic Aunt Nell will feel," because by rearranging the whole schedule for her, the hairdresser lets her know she is accepted and loved.[5]

If you happen to be the monochronic customer with the appointment, most likely you are on the verge of having a coronary as you fidget in your chair and shoot dirty looks at Aunt Nell while posting a scathing review online. But if you are a polychronic customer, you nod in approval because the hairdresser is showing proper respect to friends and family. The delay in your schedule doesn't really bother you; after all, you're probably doing something else with your time while you wait, because polychronic people are natural multitaskers. And if you *are* late for your next appointment, well...who's going to care?

That's why, for monochronic people, survival in polychronic cultures requires a conscious adjustment in time perception. The fact that you are kept waiting for an hour or two at your appointment with your attorney is not meant as an insult to you; more than likely, an esteemed acquaintance dropped in unexpectedly, and it would be unthinkably rude to rush them just because a business appointment was on the schedule.

Of course, polychronic individuals who find themselves operating in monochronic societies must also adjust their thinking about time, lest they anger all their friends and associates. But even if they train themselves to become as punctual as the clock itself, they will probably always be a little surprised at how worked up monochronics get about time. After all, time doesn't own me – it's mine to use as needed!

It's always fun to watch mixed gatherings of monochronics and polychronics. In churches where both worship together, one of the most common complaints from monochronics is that the polychronics are always late. And this is often true!

However, the monochronics are not just punctual in their arrival – they also demand to be *dismissed* punctually. Any preacher in a monochronic church knows there will come a point in his sermon when he might as well close the book and say the final amen, whether he's done or not. Why? Because regardless of whether *he* is finished, his audience is. They have moved on from listening to the message to worrying about the next item on the schedule.

Polychronics, on the other hand, are not particularly worried about what time service starts – but neither are they worried about when it ends. They did not come for a scheduled period of time...they came for the experience. Therefore, if the service runs an hour longer than usual (or if they arrive 45 minutes late), who cares? The important thing is that they are enjoying the occasion with their friends, family and church family, and they mean no disrespect whatsoever by arriving late. But why would you want to limit something so important by forcing it into a schedule?

Which approach is better? Neither, really. Each works well within its respective culture. But when cultures mingle, each should be aware of how the other operates so conflict is avoided.

When communicating with people from other cultures, be certain to educate yourself about how they view time. If their time perception is different, resist the urge to try to change it. Remember that in their culture *you* are the one who views time strangely.

I once heard of a monochronic individual who was addressing a conference in a polychronic country. He became very frustrated and lectured the attendees over their lack of punctuality, admonishing them about how inconsiderate their lateness was to the other attendees.

Given the polite and respectful nature of that particular society, no doubt he was met with earnest expressions of remorse and chagrin. To humor him, they may even have made an effort to meet his schedule expectations for the remainder of his visit. But deep down inside, they were probably somewhat perplexed at his curious fascination with time. After all, they and their entire society had been functioning just fine all their lives without being bothered by schedules!

When communicating with other cultures, nothing screams "I'm an outsider" louder than becoming irritated or obnoxious over the way they handle time. If you want to start a good conversation on your cultural CB, find out how your audience looks at the clock and adjust your own perspective accordingly. You might find that your voice is starting to shake just right!

Chapter 6: That's the Only Face You Have – Don't Lose It!

"Of course! But..."

That – or rather, its Spanish counterpart *"¡Claro! Pero..."* – is a rather common phrase in Latin America.

If Jerry and Sue are sitting in the break room at their company in Ohio (to pick a state at random) and Jerry says, "The sky is green and the grass is blue," Sue will most likely respond, "That's dumb!" – or a similarly charitable observation. But if Jerry is sitting at a coffee shop in Santiago, Chile (to pick another random place), and makes the same observation to his local host, Carlos, it wouldn't surprise me at all to hear Carlos say, "Of course! But the weather conditions have to be just right to make it look that way, because normally it's just the opposite."

Carlos knew immediately that Jerry was dead wrong. Unlike Sue, though, whose culture allows her to directly and bluntly point out the absurdity of Jerry's statement, Carlos' culture requires him to be very careful not to humiliate his friend even though he is clearly incorrect. To do so would cause him to lose status and respect – something cultural anthropologists call *losing face* – so for Carlos it might seem much more desirable to initially agree, but then gently explain why the opposite is true.

If you want to get that shake in your voice, remember that having someone from another culture agree with you does not necessarily mean they *really* agree with you. It might be that they simply don't want you to look bad.

In American society, being corrected or criticized publicly may be uncomfortable, but rarely is it considered a mortal affront. It is generally understood that a person's opinion – or even their performance – does not necessarily reflect their individual worth. But this is not the case in societies that place a high value on personal honor and status. In these societies, it may be very difficult to separate criticism of a person's performance from criticism of their value as a person. Many – if not most – collectivist, high-context and polychronic societies fall into this category, and this is especially true of those in Asia.

I remember dealing with a performance issue when I was managing my international team. Honestly, I don't even recall what the exact issue was, but I do remember that I felt the best way to handle it would be to simply talk to the whole group rather than single out the individuals who were involved. I sent an email to the group and discussed the issue without naming any names and congratulated myself on taking such a wise approach.

However, it didn't take long for one of the individuals to write back. His message was cordial, but he begged me to not take that approach again in the future. Apparently, he felt the group was aware that he was one of the culprits, and to be thus (in his mind) reprimanded in front of the group was humiliating – the exact opposite of what I intended! Instead, he asked me to speak with him privately if I had any future concerns.

This illustrates how easy it is for an intercultural communicator to miss the mark. I thought I was doing him a favor by addressing the situation vaguely and anonymously at a group level, but in his estimation I had caused him to lose face in front of all his colleagues. In America, we might just tell him to "get his big boy pants on" and deal with it – but in societies that place a lot of importance on "face," concerns like his are very real. David Ho, of the University of Hong Kong, wrote that "losing face is a serious matter which will, in varying degrees, affect one's ability to function effectively in society."[6]

When you are interacting with other cultures, be very, very careful about how you disagree. Always show respect for the other person's opinion, and if a correction is required, offer it with a heavy dose of diplomacy. But disagreements are not the only thing that can cause a loss of face. Be very cautious about using humor – especially if it involves poking fun at the other person or their culture. It is always better to make yourself the object of the joke! Or better yet, ditch the joke and choose one that is less likely to offend.

At the same time, realize that some things that are regarded as insulting in one culture may be a compliment in another, and don't be quick to take offense at perceived slights. Collectivist cultures value people, and to be accepted into the in-group is huge. When you reach that level, you are considered a close friend, and that is demonstrated by displaying intimacy. Questions that would be shocking in the United States, like "How much do you weigh?" "How old are you?" "How much do you earn?" or "How much did that cost?" show that the other person is very comfortable with you, and those things are not secrets among friends.

Some things are also perceived very differently. Americans would typically be offended at being called fat. However, in one place where we lived the ladies often told my mother, who struggled with her weight, "You're so fat!" – and they did it with a smile. The last thing they intended was to offend. Quite the contrary – many of them lived in poverty, and in their culture being chubby was a status symbol. It meant you could afford to eat! So instead of insulting her, they were admiring her beauty. See how easy it is to get yourself in trouble when you communicate across cultures?

At this point, you might be thinking, "Wow...this intercultural communication thing is a minefield!" Frankly, you're right. That's why it's not surprising that so many misunderstandings and so much gridlock occur in the business world as companies reach across borders or integrate people from different cultures into their workforces. But just because something is challenging doesn't mean it isn't worth pursuing. When we successfully weave different cultures together, we create a breathtakingly rich tapestry of human experience – well worth the effort!

Chapter 7: Keep Your Distance!

Thus far, we have depended on the analogy of truck drivers and CB radios to facilitate our discussion on intercultural communication. I'd like to take a quick detour, though, and talk about the big rigs these drivers operate.

A quick glance at my résumé is all it would take to establish that I'm neither a mechanic nor an engineer, so I'll keep my discussion of semi trucks to a very simple level that (hopefully) will not reveal my technical ignorance. But despite my limited knowledge, I think it's safe to say that semi trucks have two major components: the tractor and the trailer. These components teach us an important lesson in global leadership.

The tractor is what pulls the load. It is the smaller of the two components. The trailer is what carries the cargo and follows the lead of the tractor. On most if not all semis, the trailer makes up the bulk of the rig. However, without the tractor, the trailer really can't get its load anywhere.

This simple illustration is a terrific way of describing how leadership works. Leaders may represent a relatively small force within an organization, but things don't move ahead without them. And one interesting aspect of the tractor analogy is that, on semi rigs, tractors are always in the front. *Pushing* the trailer would probably not be a very good idea – yet another example of the fact that good leaders set the example while the organization follows behind.

Okay…enough of my leadership pep talk. You might be wondering what any of this has to do with intercultural communication. The answer is, not much – unless you happen to be a leader, supervisor or manager in a multicultural organization. If that's the case, what I'm going to share with you in this chapter is pretty important.

Let me point out one last fact about semis that might be extremely important to cross-cultural leadership. There is a proper distance that must be maintained between the tractor cab and the trailer. Too little distance and you have a collision between the two; too much distance and your trailer is probably separated from the tractor and in danger of causing a terrible accident on the highway.

A proper perspective on distance is also critical to intercultural leadership. There is, of course, the issue of physical distance that should always be kept in mind when dealing with people from other cultures; the study of *proxemics* tells us that in the United States we require about 18 to 48 inches of distance between us and other people (18 to 24 if they are close friends or relatives).[7] Anything less than this and we start feeling that – to borrow the popular expression – the other person is "getting all up in our grill." (My kids would be proud of me for knowing that line, particularly at my advanced age.) Other cultures require much less personal space, which can lead to some uncomfortable moments for those who don't realize this. But that's not really the kind of distance I'm talking about.

The distance I'm referring to is *power distance*. This refers to "the degree to which the less powerful members of a society accept and expect that power is distributed unequally" and is one of the cultural dimensions described by anthropologist Geert Hofstede.[8] In other words, power distance measures how acceptable it is in a given culture for some to have more power than others.

Generally speaking, people in the United States frown on the idea of some members of society having power over others. But in many other cultures, this is not only accepted – it's expected. The boss is the boss. He or she does not necessarily need to give an explanation for decisions made. Middle and lower management is often excluded from much of a firm's decision making, serving more to enforce what upper management has decided than to participate in actually determining the course of action.

Understanding power distance is important for ethical behavior in cross-cultural situations. In some cases, people will accept a perceived superior's opinion as fact simply because of that individual's power. Although this perception is likely decreasing as access to education and communication improve around the world, in some places people from North America and Europe are assumed to be wealthy and well educated, even if that's not really the case. Therefore, if you are a person of influence or authority, give careful consideration to what you say. It may be taken as gospel truth.

As a very young man I met a North American who had spent a significant portion of her life in another country and culture. She told me about an incident based on power distance that almost turned into an unbelievable tragedy.

She was regarded as a person of learning and authority. When a man approached her and told her his wife wanted to know how to get a complexion like the American's, the lady assumed he was joking and lightheartedly responded, "Tell her to take a bath in hydrochloric acid."

The man went on his way, and the American lady went about her business. A few minutes later, though, a terrible feeling of dread swept over her and she raced to the man's home. He was just finishing filling a tub with hydrochloric acid, and his wife would have stepped in within minutes! Thankfully, the American was able to stop him and explain that she was only kidding, and no harm was done.

The *potential* for harm, however, was indelibly branded into my brain. Unless we understand how much trust and confidence may be invested in us if we are perceived by people from power-distance-heavy cultures as superiors or authorities, we can unwittingly steer them toward disaster.

Another potential pitfall of power distance relates back to something we discussed in a previous chapter: the ability to say no. In many cultures there is an inherent difficulty to say no, resulting in what appears to outsiders to be many broken promises. Coupled with the effects of perception of power and authority, this tendency becomes even more marked. If I am from a high power distance culture, how could I possibly tell my boss no? So my American boss, who is used to employees having the cultural freedom to say "Whoa! I'm overloaded!" keeps piling more and more tasks on me, assuming that my silence or my acceptance of the tasks signals that I'm able to take them on. Meanwhile, I am overwhelmed but have no culturally acceptable way to communicate this to my superior. The inevitable outcome is that I will begin to miss deadlines and perform poorly because of my workload. I become angry at my boss for his or her insensitivity, and my boss begins to think about letting me go because I can't seem to deliver.

Getting back to the issue of space, another thing to bear in mind is that in collectivist cultures the perception of private and public spaces in life is different from what many Americans are accustomed to. In the United States, we have our "work life" and our "private life." By and large, our coworkers exist from 8-5 on weekdays, and then they disappear from our lives until time for work the next day.

In collectivist countries, however, coworkers may be regarded more as extended family. People work together during the day, and then they socialize during the evening. Many are good friends on and off the job. And because of this different way of relating to their work team, work may be conducted even outside of normal business hours. It's no surprise for a coworker to drop by your house on the weekend. And because of power distance, supervisors often become "father figures" to whom employees will resort – on and off the job – for advice with all types of situations, from work issues to family problems. But if a person from such a culture is living somewhere like the United States and drops by their department manager's home to discuss the issues they are having with their teenager, most likely they will be met with surprise and some resentment.

Of all the conflicts I saw while managing my international team, those caused by issues of power distance were among the most significant. So when managing across cultures, keep the tractor in front. Make sure the trailer is riding right where it should. And by all means, keep the shiny side up!

Chapter 8: Signing Off

There are far more factors that contribute to good intercultural communication than I could possibly cover in this book – things like past or future orientation, masculinity or femininity, etc. – but I hope by now you've begun to get a handle on developing your "trucker voice."

I'd like to suggest a few additional resources for you. To help you dig deeper, here are some of my favorite books on the subject:

- *Beyond Culture* (Edward T. Hall)
- *Cultural Anthropology* (Carol R. Ember and Melvin Ember)

- *Kiss, Bow, or Shake Hands* (Terri Morrison and Wayne A. Conaway)
- *Riding the Waves of Culture: Understanding Diversity in Global Business* (Fons Trompenaars and Charles Hampden-Turner)
- *The Art of Crossing Cultures* (Craig Storti)
- *The Dance of Life* (Edward T. Hall)
- *The Hidden Dimension* (Edward T. Hall)
- *The Silent Language* (Edward T. Hall)

These are by no means the only books on the subject, but you'll find each them to be a great read. And if you want to take a deeper look at my own research, check out my book, *Intercultural Communication in Business: How Context and Other Cultural Factors Affect Communication in Multicultural Organizations.*

Communicating across cultural lines opens the door to new friendships and rich experiences. You probably *won't* become a cultural expert overnight, but people *will* appreciate your efforts to understand them. And you'll find most people from other cultures friendly and eager to interact with you – and more like you than perhaps you realized.

It may take some practice before you get an answer on your cultural CB, so don't become discouraged. And when you *do* strike up a conversation, you may start off right and then forget the code. Or your voice may reveal the fact that you're not a truck driver. But keep trying. Pretty soon, you'll hear your voice start to shake.

Bibliography

[1] Nix, K. (2015). *Intercultural communication in business: How context and other cultural factors affect communication in multicultural organizations*. San Antonio, TX: Kelly Nix.

[2] Shannon and Weaver's model. (1949). Retrieved January 31, 2015, from http://www.oxfordreference.com/view/10.1093/oi/authority.20110803100459436

[3] Littlejohn, S. W. (2009). *Encyclopedia of Communication Theory* (Vol. 1, p. 100). Los Angeles: Sage.

[4] Hall, E. T. (1983). *The dance of life: The other dimension of time*. Garden City, NY: Anchor Press/Doubleday.

[5] Ibid.

[6] Ho, D. (1976). On the concept of face. *American Journal of Sociology, 81*(4), 867-884. Retrieved from http://www.jstor.org/stable/2777600

[7] Nolan, R. W. (1999). *Communicating and Adapting Across Culture; Living and Working in the Global Village.* Westport, CT: Bergin & Garvey. Retrieved from http://www2.pacific.edu/sis/culture/pub/1..5.2_-_Public_and_Private_.htm

[8] Hofstede, G. (n.d.). National Culture. Retrieved December 09, 2016, from https://geert-hofstede.com/national-culture.html